Art Masterpieces of
THE NATIONAL GALLERY OF ART
WASHINGTON

Designed and Produced by

TED SMART

and

DAVID GIBBON

CRESCENT

INTRODUCTION

The history of the National Gallery begins with a letter written to President Roosevelt on December 22nd 1936 by Andrew Mellon, a Pittsburgh banker and philanthropist who was Secretary to the US Treasury from 1921–1932. He was, in addition, Ambassador to Great Britain in 1932–1933 and during his stay he was so impressed by London's National Gallery that he determined himself to create an American counterpart in Washington D.C. In his letter, Mellon offered to donate his own superb collection of paintings and sculpture, to construct a suitable building to house it and to make money available to provide a much needed National Gallery of Art in the country's capital. One condition he made was that Congress should guarantee the funds needed to maintain such a gallery. Roosevelt quickly acknowledged Mellon's letter expressing his delight at such a project. The following March, Congress formally accepted Mellon's gift and a suitable site was chosen.

Today, Washington D.C.'s National Gallery of Art stands proudly between the Capitol and the Washington Monument, occupying a thirteen acre site three blocks long, on what was once a piece of marshland called Tiber Creek. It is considered to be one of the most imposing neo-classical buildings not only in Washington but in the whole of America.

The architect was John Russell Pope, whose early years of study at the American Academy in Rome clearly influenced his choice of design. A central rotunda with a huge coffered dome, colonnaded garden courts, porticos, pilasters and niches make up this beautiful building which is constructed in precious marbles. Pink Tennessee marble arranged so that the darkest blocks are nearest to the ground, the lightest at the top, imperial green marble from a quarry near Lucca for the columns of the dome and floors of green marble from Vermont.

Sadly, Pope died in the very year, 1937, that work began on the Gallery but fortunately his partners Otto R. Eggers and David Paul Higgins carried out his plans as he would have wished. The cost of the building was reputed to be fifteen million dollars; the value of the collections it contains priceless.

The works of art are thoughtfully displayed, each one given sufficient space and protected by an air conditioning system that maintains the required temperature and humidity and filters the outside air, thereby removing harmful atmospheric agents. To preserve the fine colours from fading the windows are fitted with plastic filters in order to screen the ultraviolet rays. Restoration is a continual process that keeps the collections in prime condition.

So that visitors can appreciate the contents of the Gallery fully, plenty of seats are provided and a cafeteria is available for refreshment. In addition, orchestral concerts and displays of rare flowers make full use of the pleasant garden courts. For those who wish for information about the exhibitions, expert guides are at hand and lectures, films and a comprehensive library are constantly available to provide specialist knowledge.

The National Gallery is one of the youngest major galleries in the world. Andrew Mellon's fine collection of 17th Century Dutch and 18th Century English paintings, Italian Renaissance sculpture and numerous examples of American art formed the basis of the Gallery's exhibits but other magnificent collections were to follow.

One was given by the Widener family, a collection started by Peter A. B. Widener of Philadelphia, a banker and railway magnate at the end of the 19th Century. Works by eminent English artists like Reynolds, Gainsborough, Turner and Constable, Italian Renaissance masterpieces from the 16th Century, valuable sculpture, Chinese porcelain and exquisite tapestries are just a part of the most generous gift.

Pennsylvanian Samuel Henry Kress, a one time school teacher, purchased a small stationery shop near his birthplace and eventually became the wealthy owner of two hundred and sixty five stores across the country. At the age of sixty five he became extremely interested in art and in 1929, using part of his large fortune, created the Kress Foundation which was added to in 1940 by his brother Claude's estate. When Samuel Kress died at the age of ninety two, his younger brother Rush Harrison became president of the Foundation which contained works of art from all the important European Schools. Part of the massive Kress collection is in the National Gallery and part in various other museums.

The field of Modern Art, especially the French Impressionists, the cubists and the Fauvists, fascinated Chester Dale, a New York banker, and his first wife Maud. The Dale Collection first came to the National Gallery in the form of extensive loans, until his death in 1962 when the entire collection was left to the Gallery in his will.

Represented at the Gallery is a specialised branch of art – the graphic arts – containing about 22,000 prints, drawings and water colours, largely the gift of the Rosenwald Collection. Like many of the great benefactors of the Gallery, Lessing K. Rosenwald was from Pennsylvania, the chairman of a chain of department stores who was both a selective and an enthusiastic collector of graphic art and became an expert in his field. His discriminatory purchases included over seven hundred 15th century wood and copper engravings by such artists as Dürer and Lucas Van Leydon and many valuable water colours. The Rosenwald Collection is housed in a specially built museum near Philadelphia but it is at the disposal of the National Gallery where a number of rooms for exhibitions are reserved.

Some of the major collections have been specifically mentioned in this introduction but throughout the years gifts of money, and actual exhibits, large and small, have been donated to the National Gallery, thereby ensuring that one of the world's finest homes of art treasures can continue to acquire works of the greatest importance and maintain them to the very highest standard.

Illustrated *left* is 'A Girl with a Watering Can' by Pierre-Auguste **Renoir** (1841-1919).

Duccio di Buoninsegna (c. 1255–1319), a contemporary of Giotto, was of the Sienese school; his work reflects much of the Byzantine tradition which is strongly reflected in the heavy, gold background of 'The Calling of the Apostles Peter and Andrew' *below.* His expressive figures reveal his strong pictorial ability, and his quiet refinement shows the outstanding skill of this great artist.

The triptych *above right*, 'Madonna Enthroned with Saints and Angels' is the work of the Florentine painter, Agnolo **Gaddi** (c. 1333–1396). A pupil of the master, Giotto, Agnolo's work was both influential and prolific. Early in his career he worked in the Vatican, with his brother, Giovanni, executing a number of frescoes for Pope Urban V. Some of his most outstanding works, consisting of a series of frescoes in the choir of Sta Croce, in Florence, reveal, by the emphasis placed on composition, a new approach to the International Gothic style.

The magnificent tondo 'The
Adoration of the Magi' *overleaf left* is
the work of the eminent Florentine
artist Fra **Angelico** (Guido di Pietro)
(c. 1400-1455), and his coadjutant, Fra
Filippo **Lippi** (c. 1406-1469).
Angelico was born in Vecchio and
adopted the name of Fra Giovanni da
Fiesole when he entered the
Dominican convent in 1421. His
paintings were deeply religious in
essence and reflect his great faith and
innate gentleness.

Domenico di Tommaso Bigordi)
Ghirlandaio (c. 1449-1494), who
painted the 'Madonna and Child'
overleaf right, is renowned for his
detailed frescoes; particularly
noteworthy are those in the Sta
Trinità and Sta Maria Novella,
Florence.

'Crucifixion' *right* is by the Sienese
artist **Benvenuto** di Giovanni (c. 1436-
1518).

The beautifully detailed painting 'The Adoration of the Magi' illustrated *below* is by Sandro Filipepi **Botticelli** (about 1445-1510), a pupil of Lippi and one of the greatest of the Florentine early Renaissance painters; his work embodies the new spirit of the era. A substantial amount of his ornamentation was spent on ecclesiastical undertakings and included work for many of the major Florentine churches; and his numerous private commissions, particularly those of the powerful Medici family, brought him considerable success and rich rewards.

Agnolo Degli **Erri** lived in Emilia, Italy, in the second half of the 15th century, where he executed the panel 'A Dominican Preaching' *right*. Although the painting shows some signs of past mutilation, the density of the colour has withstood the passage of time.

The picture portrays a friar of the Dominican order instructing his flock in the Christian doctrine. The order was founded in 1215 by St Dominic, who was originally from the Spanish diocese of Osma, and he gave his followers a code based on that of St Augustine. This innovation empowered the confrères to instruct the masses, which had previously been the prerogative of the bishops. From its inception the order has been a combining of both the active and contemplative aspects of the ministry.

Giovanni **Bellini** (about 1430–1516), the son of Jacopo Bellini, was influential in the development of Venetian art and became the foremost painter of his period. His workshop was noted for its devotional pictures of the Madonna, and the mellow richness of Bellini's work is clearly evident in the two 'Madonna and Child' painting illustrated *below and right:* both pictures evoke a feeling of great sensitivity and gentleness, for which this gifted artist is renowned.

'The Holy Family' *left* is the work of **Giorgione** (Giorgio da Castelfranco) (about 1476–1510) and although little is known of the short life of this talented man his artistry was to have a profound influence on the great Titian.

'The Nativity' *below left* is characteristic of the style of the Flemish artist, Petrus **Christus** (c. 1420–1472/3), who incorporated in much of his work some of the traditions of Early Netherlandish art. It is believed that he was responsible for the introduction of geometric perspective into the Lowlands; his pre-occupation with the definition of space is illustrated in his composition of the 'Virgin with SS Jerome and Francis', the first Netherlandish painting to reveal a single vanishing point.

'The Small Cowper Madonna' *left* is by **Raphael** Santi (c. 1483–1520), who ranks amongst the greatest artists of the Italian High Renaissance. His early career began as an assistant to the Perugino, from where he moved to Florence. In 1508 he went to Rome, where he was employed Pope Julius II to redecorate a number of rooms the Vatican. This gifted painter is particularly renowned for his gentle Madonna interpretation and on his premature death, at the age of 37, his assistants were able to continue the work of their great master.

Titian's (Tiziano Vecellio) (about 1487/90–157 powerful skill as an outstanding craftsman matured during the long life of this man of geniu who was to influence many artists, including bot Tintoretto and Veronese. Numbered amongst th patrons who provided Titian with many commissions were Phillip II of Spain and the Holy Roman Emperor, Charles V. 'Alfonso d'Este and Laura Diante' *below* is an allegorical painting, one of a series of three, painted for Alfonso d'Este.

A new feeling for beauty revived the declining Sienese school in the late 15th and early 16th centuries, through the works of artists such as, Matteo di Giovanni, Neroccio de'Landi and **Benvenuto di Giovanni** (c. 1436–1518). The meticulously detailed cusped panel, 'The Adoration of the Magi', a detail of which is show *left*, indicates Benvenuto's masterly construction and superb use of light and colour.

Bronzino (Agnolo di Cosimo di Mariano) (1503–1572), as Court Painter, executed many portraits of the Medici family, in the formal style favoured by the Mannerists of the period. 'A Young Woman and her little Boy', illustrated *righ* displays the high degree of finish and bright colours, characteristic of the artist's work.

Giovanni-Battista **Tiepolo** (1696-1770) was the last of the great Venetian decorators and his painting 'Apollo Pursuing Daphne' *above* reveals the grace and elegance which is typical of Rococo art.

'Portrait of a Young Lady as Venus Binding the Eyes of Cupid' *right* is a further outstanding example of the work of **Titian**.

Lucas **Cranach** the Elder (1472-1553), the great painter of the German Reformation met, at Wittenberg, Martin Luther, with whom he developed a close and enduring friendship. An excellent portrait painter, Cranach pioneered full-length figure painting in German art, and much of his work is invested in mythological themes, admirably illustrated in 'The Nymph of the Spring' *left*.

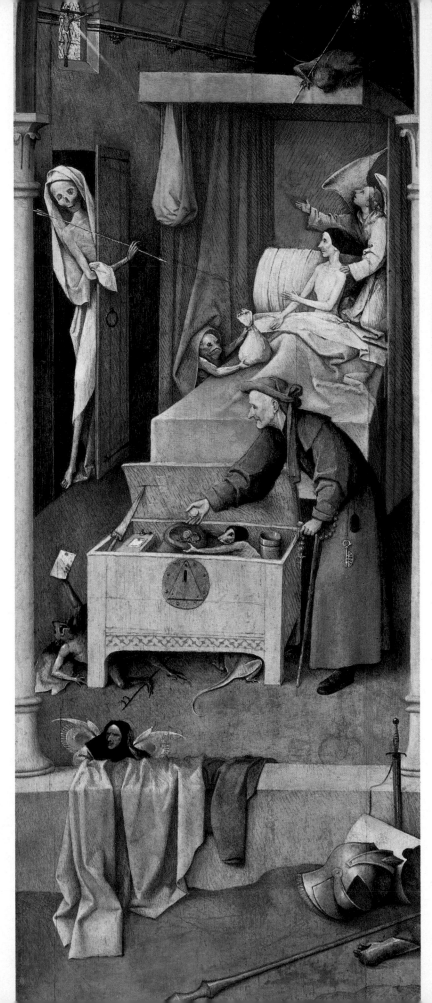

The nephew of Canaletto, Bernardo **Bellotto** (c. 1720-1780), whose meticulous paintings were used by architects to reconstruct Warsaw after the city's destruction in the Second World War, had made Warsaw his home under the patronage of King Stanislas Poniatowski. Bellotto's precision and careful detailing are apparent in his rendition of 'The Castle of Nymphenburg', *above*.

The work of Hieronymus **Bosch** (c. 1450-60-1516) often includes macabre and grotesque figures, as illustrated in 'Death and the Miser' *left*. This highly original Flemish artist spent his working life in the northern Netherlands, and although he painted many nightmarish scenes, the majority of his work consisted of religious subjects. His paintings are superbly executed; his discriminate use of colour imbuing his paintings with a shining brilliance.

Giovanni Paolo **Pannini**'s (c. 1691-1765) early study of the art of perspective led to his recognition as the foremost artist of Roman topography in the 18th century, and in 1732 he became the professor of perspective at the French Academy. One of the most famous of his interior views is the 'Interior of St Peters, Rome' shown *right*. Pannini's success resulted in many requests for his paintings, and his delicate treatment is indicative of French Rococo art.

The last of the great masters of the Bruges school, Gerard **David** (c. 1460-1523), was renowned for his superb altarpieces, which includes the triptych *above*, the 'Saint Anne Altarpiece'. His rigid style is tempered by a rich use of colour, with carefully composed utilization of light and space.

Mabuse (Jan Gossaert) (c. 1478-1532), whose adopted name was derived from his birthplace, Mauberge, in northern France, was a noted Flemish artist who ranked among the first painters to pioneer the art of the Italian Renaissance in the Netherlands. 'Portrait of a Banker' *left* is a fine example of Mabuse's outstanding ability in portraiture and denotes the artist's psychological insight, with particular emphasis placed on the expressiveness of the hands.

'The Small Crucifixion' *right* is an important work by Matthias **Grünewald** (1455-80-1528) who is considered to be one of the greatest German painters of his era. After his appointment as Court Painter to the Archbishop of Mainz, he received several important commissions, including the altarpiece of the Antonite monastery, deemed to be his masterpiece.

Peter Paul **Rubens** (c. 1577-1640), a master who is still revered for his originality and dynamism, was a traditional in both his art and religion. 'The Gerbier Family' *above* is a splendid example of his work.

Noted for his winter scenes, the Dutch artist Hendrick **Avercamp** (c. 1585-1634), was born in Amsterdam but spent the majority of his life in Campin. 'A Scene on the Ice' *above left* is typical of Avercamp's style.

One of the most skilful landscape artists of his era, Aelbert **Cuyp** (c. 1620-1691) contributed greatly to the Dutch realism of the period. 'The Maas at Dordrecht' *left*, with its delicate, golden hues, shows the outstanding ability of this brilliant painter and is indicative of the influence of Claude.

'The Bedroom' *right* is the work of the Dutch artist Pieter de **Hooch** (c. 1629-after 1684), a Baroque genre painter of the Delft school, noted for his small canvasses of interior scenes which he executed with perfect precision.

The famous Dutch artist **Rembrandt** van Rijn (c. 1606-1669), included, in his vast repertoire of paintings, a superb collection of portraiture. This master of chiaroscuro was influenced by Elsheimer, who had introduced him to the technique developed by Caravaggio, and also by Pieter Lastman, under whose studio direction he had worked. Included in the Gallery are the three magnificent portraits illustrated: *left*, 'Self-Portrait', *above right*, 'Study of an Old Man' and *overleaf left*, 'Portrait of a Gentleman with a Tall Hat and Gloves'.

'The Hermit' *above* is by Gerrit **Dou** (c. 1613-1675), the son of a Leyden glazier, whose early training had included glass-engraving. Although his early paintings were influenced by Rembrandt, with whom he had studied, his later work was mainly composed of domestic genre studies, with particular emphasis on still-life subjects.

'Ships in the Scheldt Estuary' *right* is the work of the Circle of Hendrick van **Anthonissen**, active in Holland about 1606-1654-60.

The charming study of 'Susanna Fourment and her Daughter' *overleaf right* is just one of the Gallery's fine collection by Antony van **Dyck** (c. 1599-1641). This Flemish artist, whose early career was dominated by the dramatic style of Rubens, is noted for his prolific portraiture of European nobility. In 1632 he returned to England and received a knighthood from Charles I, who also appointed him Court Painter.

'The Sacrament of the Last Supper' *above* was painted in 1955 by the Surrealist artist Salvador **Dali** (1904-   ). Early in his career Dali absorbed a number of styles, ranging from the 19th century Romantic to the Italian Metaphysical painters; but in the late 1920's he was strongly influenced by the theories of Freud and his association with the Paris Surrealists, which brought about his fascination with subconscious imagery. Dali's versatility, however, led to his spending a considerable amount of time, during the 1940's, in designing jewellery, theatre sets and the interiors of fashionable shops. In the period between 1950-70, Dali's preoccupation lay mainly in painting religious subjects, into which category the 'Last Supper' falls.

The dramatic application of colour and elongated shapes of 'Laocoön' (a detail of which is shown) *left* are indicative of the visionary style of **El Greco** (Doménicos Theotocópoulos) (c. 1540-1614), which is a mature work by this highly original artist. His earlier work was influenced by the Venetian painters, particularly Tintoretto, but by the mid-1580's, after his establishment at Toledo, he developed his own personal approach which was met with approbation by the intellectuals and ecclesiastics of the city.

Pablo **Picasso** (c. 1881-1973) is universally acknowledged to have produced the profoundest impact on 20th century art. His basic concept, of involving the spectator in his compositions, has been a determining factor of his work. 'The Lovers' *right* was painted during the artist's 'neo-classical' period.

'The Repentant Magdalen' *above* is characteristic of the style of Georges de **La Tour** (c. 1593-1652) whose candlelight subjects express his originality in both colour and form. It is interesting to note that the artist made replicas of almost every one of his authenticated works.

Illustrated *left*, 'Diane de Poitiers', is the work of François **Clouet** (?-1572) who, with his father Jean, was considered to be amongst the finest French painters at the Court of Fontainebleau. The painting, however, has been variously considered to be that of Marie Touchet, the mistress of Charles IX.

Jean-Antoine **Watteau** (c. 1684-1721) introduced to French society his gentle, ethereal paintings which often contained an atmosphere of deep melancholy. This innovative style, known as the 'fêtes-galantes', transported the mundanity of life into an earthly paradise. His early training had included the development of Rococo design; and he used his large collection of drawings as a basis for his delicate paintings. 'The Italian Comedians' *right* is a splendid example of his work.

The work of François **Boucher** (c. 1703-1770) epitomises fully French Rococo art during the 18th century. Boucher's talent was multi-faceted, for not only did he execute a vast number of paintings, but he was also an engraver, decorator and an inspector of the Gobelin tapestry factory. He became First Painter to the king, under Louis XV, and amongst the most notable of his pupils was the king's mistress, Madame de Pompadour. His exquisitely modelled forms and subtle colouring is evidenced in both the portrait of 'Mme Bergeret' *right* and 'The Love Letter' *below*.

Charles Amédée-Philippe van **Loo** (c. 1719-1795) painted the charming composition *left*, 'The Magic Lantern'.

One of the last great artists to work in the French Rococo style, Jean-Honoré **Fragonard** (c. 1732-1806), received his early training from Chardin and then Boucher. Most of his works consist of portraits, landscapes, and 'fêtes-galantes', after the manner of Watteau, and are characterized by their romantic settings and sensitive approach. 'A Young Girl Reading' *right* and 'The Happy Family' *above left* are just two of the Gallery's impressive collection of Fragonard's compositions.

The charming 'Group Portrait' *above* is a canvas by François-Hubert **Drouais** (c. 1727-1775), a fashionable portraitist of the 18th century. François was a pupil of his father, Hubert Drouais, an artist who specialized in miniatures.

'A Painter's Studio' *left* is an elegant composition by Louis-Léopold **Boilly** (c. 1761-1845), a prolific painter and noted lithographer, who is primarily known for his satirical portrayals of Parisian manners during the time of the Revolution and French Empire.

A superb example of the work of Théodore **Géricault** (c. 1791-1824), 'Trumpeters of Napoleon's Imperial Guard' illustrated *overleaf left*, shows the artist's outstanding ability to portray animal movement with apparent ease. Géricault's death, as the result of a fall from a horse, tragically brought to a close his brief, yet accomplished, career.

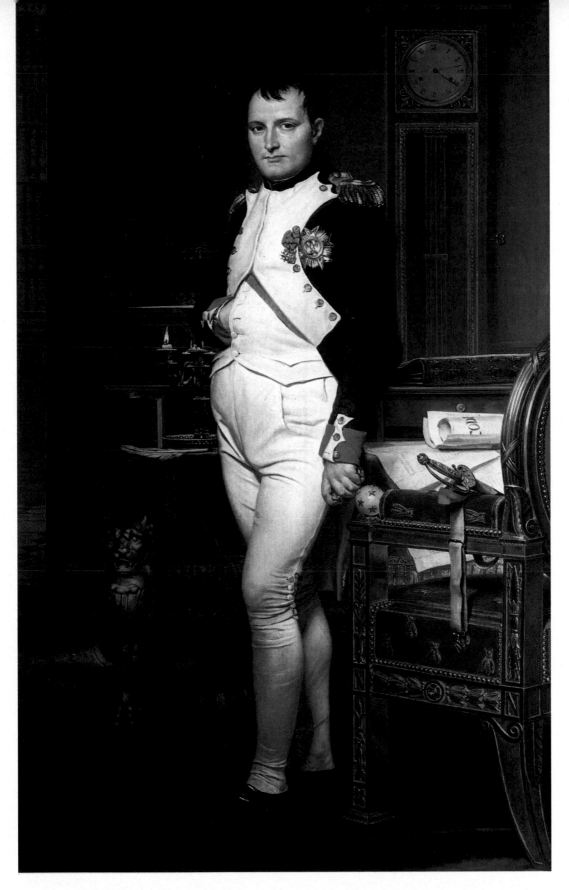

Jacques-Louis **David** (c. 1748-1825), the appointed painter to Napoleon, was responsible for many of the official portraits of the régime; 'Napoleon in his Study' *above* being an excellent example of his distinguished portraiture. His magnificent history paintings denote David's devotion to the Neoclassical and antique ideals, whilst his pre-eminence as a teacher was to influence, in particular, his favourite pupil, Gros.

The work of Jean-Baptiste-Camille **Corot** (c. 1796-
..75) was influential in the development of the
..pressionist movement; his natural landscapes,
..th their simple blending of clear colours,
..ticipate the Impressionist's move away from any
..mantic pre-conceptions towards a more realistic
..proach. Illustrated *left* is a charming study entitled
..he Artist's Studio', whilst the tranquil scene *above*
..picting the 'Ville D'Avray' reveals Corot's perfect
..rmony with nature.

..gène **Boudin** (c. 1824-1898), although not an
..iginal member of the Impressionists, nevertheless
..hibited with the group in 1874. He painted a large
..mber of beach scenes, amongst them 'On the
..ach' *right*, and 'The Beach at Deauville' *overleaf*
..ttom left*, whilst his fascination for the sea led him to
..ake careful notes of the prevailing conditions on
..e reverse of his paintings. Boudin was influential in
..rsuading the young Monet to develop his
..ndscape compositions and his inspiration is later
..ident in Monet's work.

The Gallery contains a magnificent collection of 19th century paintings and illustrated on these pages are some superb examples.

Above left: a detail from 'Rocks in the Forest of Fontainebleau' by Jean-Baptiste-Camille **Corot** (c. 1796-1875).

Left: 'Before the Ballet' by Hilaire-Germain-Edgar **Degas** (c. 1834-1917).

Above: 'Self-Portrait' by Henri **Fantin-Latour** (c. 1836-1904).

Below: 'Advice to a Young Artist' by Honoré **Daumier** (c. 1808-1879).

Above right: 'At the Races' by Édouard **Manet** (c. 1832-1883).

Right: 'Banks of the Oise' by Alfred **Sisley** (c. 1839-1899).

Claude **Monet** (c. 1840-1926), the innovator of the Impressionist movement, was greatly influenced by Boudin, the precursor of open-air painting. The Impressionists sought to portray the naturalness of the landscape, placing particular emphasis on the effects produced by the qualities of light and atmosphere. The movement was initially met with derision, for the 'Establishment' expected art to conform to the idealised forms and high narrative content previously thought to be the only acceptable mode of painting. Spontaneity, hence the desire to paint directly in front of the subject matter, particularly out of doors, was a primary factor governing the group, whilst the emotional involvement was also considered to be an integral part of obtaining the desired results, those of freshness and vitality.

'Waterloo Bridge, Gray Day' *above* and 'Rouen Cathedral, West Façade, Sunlight' *left* are two outstanding examples of Monet's work.

'The Artist's Father' *right* is by Paul **Cézanne** (c. 1839-1906), an artist who is generally linked to the Impressionist movement, but who is considered to be amongst the greatest of the 'Post-Impressionist' painters.

Maurice Utrillo. V.

Paul **Gauguin** (c. 1848-1903) strove to convey his 'beautiful thoughts' through the medium of art, by his use of bold, rich colour. His desire to obtain a simplicity, akin to folk-art, led him eventually to the South Pacific where he spent a considerable amount of time, particularly in Tahiti, the Marquesas Islands and Martinique. 'Self-Portrait' *above* is dated 1889.

Henri de **Toulouse-Lautrec** (c. 1864-1901), influenced by Degas and Japanese prints, captured so magnificently the Parisian world of night-life, portraying the singers and performers of the day, and is especially renowned for the superb collection of posters he produced, executed with panache and outstanding draughtsmanship. Included in the Gallery's extensive range of his work are: 'Quadrille at the Moulin Rouge' *above right* and 'Alfred La Guigne' *right*.

'The Church of Saint Severin' *left* is a noted example of the work of Maurice **Utrillo** (c. 1883-1955), which belongs to the artist's 'white period', during which he produced some of his finest paintings. In spite of his life-long battle against alcoholism, Utrillo created a plethora of oil paintings, including the many street scenes of Montmartre, for which he is primarily known.

Vincent **Van Gogh** (c. 1853-1890) became attached to the Impressionist movement after his arrival in Paris, in 1886, and produced some of the group's most intense paintings. The son of a Dutch pastor, his deep sensitivity and compassion compelled him, in his early years, to seek fulfilment in the Church. However, in 1880, he began to draw and from this point developed his artistic passion intending to serve mankind through the medium of art. His brief and tortured career lasted for only ten years, until he committed suicide in July 1890.

'The Olive Orchard' *above,* with its short, curving brushstrokes, reveals the underlying tension so often apparent in Van Gogh's work. 'Girl in White' *right* is a sombre composition, painted only a month before the artist's death.

One of the most brilliant members of the Impressionist school, Pierre-Auguste **Renoir** (c. 1841-1919), was principally concerned with figure painting, rather than with the landscapes favoured by his contemporaries. He was apprenticed, at the age of 13, to a porcelain manufacturer and his growing interest in art led him to take painting lessons from the Swiss artist Charles Gleyre. The young Renoir, however, developed a close affinity with Sisley, Monet and Bazille, and together they worked towards a freer, more naturalistic approach, which was to result in the Impressionist movement.

Renoir's brushwork and application of pure colour are beautifully illustrated in 'Oarsmen at Chatou' *above* and 'The Vintagers' *right*. 'Girl with a Basket of Fish' *far left* and 'Girl with a Basket of Oranges' *near left* are indicative of Renoir's later work, painted during the period when he had temporarily rejected Impressionism, and they reveal the classicism brought about by his study of Raphael.

Two further outstanding examples of **Renoir**'s work from the Gallery's comprehensive collection are shown *left*, 'Odalisque' and *above*, 'Diana'.
'Still Life' *above left* is the work of André **Derain** (c. 1880-1954) and, although an original member of the Fauve movement, his later style remained closer to the Postimpressionists rather than to the evolving Cubism of the period. Drawn by traditionalism, Derain, throughout his life admired and studied the art of the old masters, which was to have a profound effect upon his work.

'Odalisque with Raised Arms' *left* is the work of Henri **Matisse** (c. 1869-1954) who led the first modern movement of 20th century art, known as Fauvism. The reference to 'fauves' (beasts) was made by the critic Louis Vauxcelles, during the exhibition of the 1905 Salon, in his comparison of the wild, frenzied colours of the paintings, with the more sober, conservative sculpture.

Influenced greatly by Matisse, Raoul **Dufy** (c. 1877-1953), did much to popularise Fauvism by his paintings containing rich and vibrant colours. His later work, however, typified in 'Reclining Nude' *above* reveals the extent to which he developed his own personal style.

Georges **Braque** (c. 1882-1963) who, with Picasso, was instrumental in founding the Cubist movement, revolutionised the art-world by a totally new approach to painting. In 'Still-Life-Le Jour' *right* Braque conveys clearly recognisable forms without resorting to imitation and invites the spectator to become actively involved in his art.

'The Ragan Sisters' *above left*, a lovely example of the work of Jacob **Eichholtz** (c. 1776-1842), is just one of the Gallery's extensive collection by this fine portraitist.

George **Romney** (c. 1734-1802), a fashionable 18th century portrait painter of English society, succeeded in acquiring a large clientele by his ability to portray his sitters in a gentile and flattering guise. 'Miss Willoughby' *above* is indicative of Romney's preference for classical poses and subtle use of colour.

Thomas **Gainsborough** (c. 1727-1788), whose name is synonymous with the glories of British portraiture during the Georgian period, is believed to have painted the portrait of 'The Honourable Mrs Graham' *right* in 1755. Although he is primarily noted for his portraiture, he nevertheless produced many idyllic landscape scenes and on occasion would create miniature sets in his studio from which he worked.

Benjamin **West** (c. 1738-1820), whose self-portrait is illustrated *left*, was a founding member of the Royal Academy, and history painter to George III. This highly talented man spent the greater part of his life in London, where he enjoyed the patronage of the king until 1801.

The fine portrait of 'George Washington' *left* is the work of the gifted American portraitist, Gilbert **Stuart** (c. 1755-1828). The painting, known as the 'Vaughan-Sinclair portrait', is a replica of an earlier study.

A pupil of Stuart, Thomas **Sully** (c. 1783-1872), was born in England and moved to the U.S. in 1792. A prodigious portrait painter, his elegant style and warm mellow tones are evidenced in the detail from the portrait of 'Andrew Jackson' *above*.

'Alexander Hamilton' *above right* is by the distinguished artist John **Trumbull** (c. 1756-1843) who faithfully recorded, on canvas, the major events of the American Civil War. This talented man was also an author and architect and his designs included those of the Trumbull Gallery at Yale.

John Singleton **Copley** (c. 1738-1815), one of the greatest American artists of the 18th century, moved from Boston to London in 1755, where he was elected to the Royal Academy in 1779. 'Watson and the Shark' *right* is regarded as his first important work.

The Gallery's magnificent collection of paintings includes some notable representations by eminent 18th and 19th century artists, and includes the splendid examples illustrated on these pages.

Above left: 'Mrs Paul Smith and her Twins' by Erastus Salisbury **Field** (c. 1805-1900).

Above: a detail from 'The Hoppner Children' by John **Hoppner** (c. 1758-1810).

Above right: 'The Cornell Farm' by Edward **Hicks** (c. 1780-1849).

Left: 'Flax Scutching Bee' by Linton **Park** (c. 1826--1906).

Right: 'Mount Vernon' by George **Ropes** (c. 1788-1819).

'The White Girl' *left* is one of the most famous of the early paintings by James Abbott McNeill **Whistler** (c. 1834-1903) and portrays his mistress, Joanna Heffernan. This full-length portrait won considerable acclaim for the artist when it was exhibited at the Paris Salon des Refusés, in 1863. Born in Massachusetts, Whistler spent his early years in Russia, where his father was employed as a civil engineer. After the family's return to America, he went on to attend the Military Academy at West Point, but realising his ambition to become an artist, abandoned the army and moved first to Paris where he commenced his studies. He spent the remainder of his life in Europe, settling in London in 1863, and his superb scenes of nocturnal London are considered to be amongst the greatest of his works. This versatile artist was also a skilful etcher and lithographer, and a noted theorist on art; whilst in his later years his colourful personality made him a leading figure in London society.

'The Notch of the White Mountains' (Crawford Notch) *above right* and 'The Voyage of Life: Youth' *right* are two outstanding examples of the romantic landscapes created by Thomas **Cole** (c. 1801-1848), a founder of the Hudson River school.
As a basis for his paintings, Cole used the pencil sketches he made whilst travelling extensively in the Northeast, and these were particularly useful to him during the winter months as he worked in his studio.
John Trumbull and Asher Durand were instrumental in furthering Cole's career, for they had purchased some of his landscapes which they had seen exhibited in a shop window in New York. The patrons they brought him helped to ensure his success.

Mary **Cassatt** (c. 1844-1926), although
an American by birth, spent much of
her early life in Europe. A close friend
of Degas, Mary was strongly
influenced by him and exhibited with
the Impressionists on several
occasions. Her work, however, is
highly original and she developed her
own personal style, being particularly
imaginative in the use of pastels.
Primarily a figure painter, her initial
compositions consisted of groups,
whilst in later works she concentrated
on portraying the special relationship
between mothers and their children.
'Girl Arranging her Hair' *left,*
'Children Playing on the Beach' *above*
and 'Mother and Child' *above right,*
display Mary's outstanding artistic
qualities.

John Singer **Sargent** (c. 1856-1925)
was born in Florence of American
parents, establishing his American
citizenship in 1876. After studying in
Paris and Madrid he settled in
London, where he became a
fashionable Edwardian portraitist. In
later life he devoted his time to
painting murals and landscapes,
which he executed in watercolour.
'Repose' *right* was painted in 1911.

Representative of 19th century American art
are the paintings: *above*, 'Bareback Riders' by
W. H. **Brown** (19th century); *left*, 'Snow
Flurries' by Andrew Newell **Wyeth** (1917–   );
and *above right* 'The City from Greenwich
Village' by John French **Sloan** (c. 1871–1951).

The powerful, vivid paintings of Winslow
Homer (c. 1836–1910), depicting marine
subjects, are amongst the finest of late-19th-
century American art. Homer used both
watercolours and oils to express his deep
preoccupation with the sea and 'Breezing Up'
right is a splendid example of his work.

'Red Rose Cantata' *overleaf* is the work of Alma
W. **Thomas**.

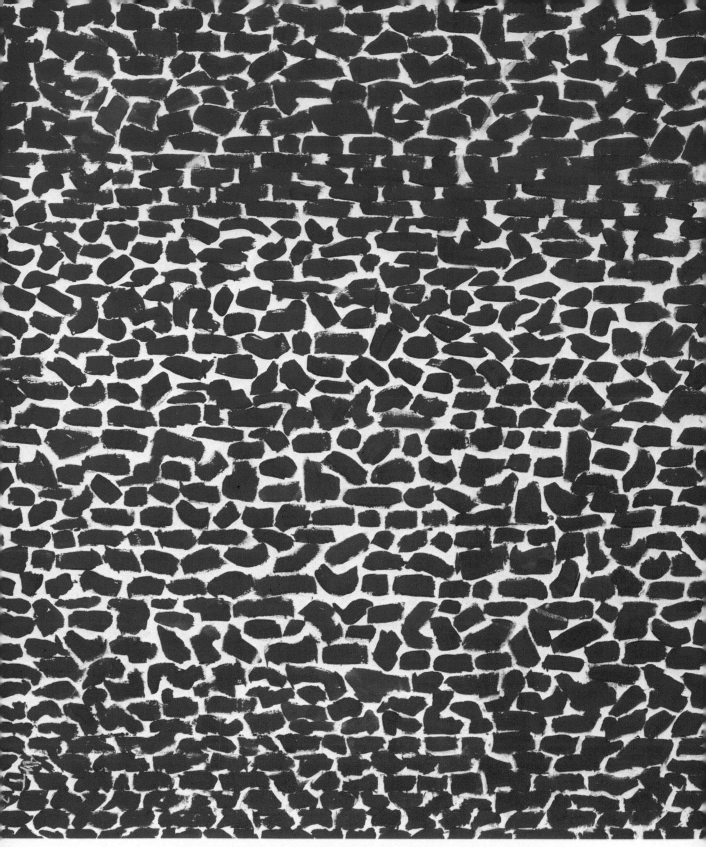

First published in Great Britain 1979 by Colour Library International Ltd.
© Illustrations: Jack Novak/Foto Salmer, Barcelona, Spain.
Colour separations by FERCROM, Barcelona, Spain.
Display and text filmsetting by Focus Photoset, London, England.
Printed and bound by L.E.G.O. Vicenza, Italy.
Published by Crescent Books, a division of Crown Publishers Inc.
All rights reserved.
Library of Congress Catalogue Card No. 78-72969
CRESCENT 1979